DE LAN'

Guh back to de lan' muh boy
It clothe yuh
feed yuh
It gih yuh yuh very life
Don' despise it
Love it
Yuh were made for it
Don' yuh remembah
back in Africa
We an' the black earth was one
We liked ta touch it
work it
dig it
It mek we rich
an' it mek we poor
Listen muh boy this here lan' will never die
decline
but neveh die
'cause this is a god a man a woman a tree
this lan' is wata
fiah
this lan' is eveah ting
this lan' is before we now
and after
Guh back muh boy it is yuh heritage
yuh proud heritage
yuh rich proud black heritage
Don' be shame fuh it
yuh belong to it
an' it belong to you.

— *Marita Browne*

Ragged Point

Accra Beach

St. Nicholas Abbey

Animal Flower Cave

THE ISLAND
BARBADOS

PHOTOGRAPHED BY DAN DRY

WEST INDIA PUBLISHERS LTD.
in association with
HARMONY HOUSE PUBLISHERS - LOUISVILLE

Executive Editors: William Butler and William Strode
Director of Photography: William Strode
First Edition printed Summer 1988 by West India Publishers Ltd.
in association with Harmony House Publishers - Louisville
Manufactured in Spain through Four Colour Imports, Louisville, Kentucky
Hardcover International Standard Book Number 0-916509-50-8
Library of Congress Number 88-082036

Additional photography by Tony Arruza, page 97; William Strode, pages 114-115;
Willie Alleyne, page 122, top; and Ronnie Carrington, page 122, bottom.

West India Publishers is pleased to be associated with
this publication, *The Island: Barbados.* The photographs and
the text have been judiciously interwoven to present an
authentic and exciting portrait of Barbados.

So frequently, one finds that true and fresh perceptions are
brought to a place or subject matter by those who are indeed
new to that place and subject. Here, we have been afforded a
Barbados that looks spectacularly new, even in some of our
older and more familiar locations.

Over the past decade, there has been an increasing awareness
in Barbados of the island's heritage, as expressed both in its
man-made and natural environment; and in this respect,
Barbados is in step with a global trend.

A journey through this new publication will be an exciting
extension of that awarenesss.

ISLAND DAY

Coral.
       Rock.
              Sandstone.
Feel the words on your tongue.

Coral.
       Rock.
              Shell.
Shells.
Sea-shells.
Hear the surge of the surf on the Bathsheba beach,
the ebb and the flow of the tide of our hearts.

Shell.
       Rock.
              Wood.

Driftwood.
Piece of mahogany smoothed by the sea
brown bathed in blues everchanging
turquoise to ultramarine.

Rock.
       Wood.
              Tree.
Coconuts fringe the shore where the sun rises, their leaves
rustling in the wind.
In the fields of St. Philip the cotton flowers are yellow;
the scent of the balsam clings to the breeze below Cliff.

Coral.
       Rock.
              Earth.
In valleys green with cane the soil is black
and red is the clay on the hill.
The earth turns like the potter's wheel
and long is the labour of man

in the cane-fields edged with khus-khus grass whose roots smell
sweet as the juice of the cane
in the cane-fields edged with pea-bushes whose flower are yellow
not the yellow of the cotton flowers,
or that of the crocus which grows in the ditch

in the towns
in the factories
in the banks and the stores and the offices

in the towns
where the roar of traffic cannot drown
the sound of typewriters in air-conditioned rooms
the sound of telex-machines and cash-registers
the sound of the making of money.

On top of a cliff in St. Lucy
an old man smites the ground with a rod of iron
digging crabs for bait.

Another old man climbs the cliff with his burden:
a bucket of sand.

St. Peter was a fisherman
and home the ice-boats come
"Fish! Fish! Four for a dollar!"
And all along the coast
ice-cubes in tourists' glasses
tinkle now their Angelus.

A piece of rab land in St. Thomas
brightens with the flight of grass canaries
As the sun sets
golden in glory
pinking the clouds
warriors binding their wounds in the night.

–John Gilmore

ISLAND NIGHT

Rush-hour minibuses, dub-music blasting,
hurtle past
city-street
sellers
who call out their wares

opening coconuts with
three
deft
chops
of a machete.

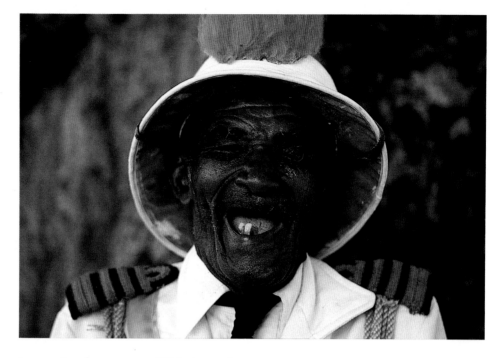

Night falls
and
the beaters
and the shakers
of the tambourines
gather round the fervour of the preacher in the clap-
hand
church.

Saturday night down the shop.
On a white china plate ringed with tomato
chunks of black sausage are laid out
with pieces of ears and feet in lime and salt
with flecks of green cucumber
and small, small peppers
hot like fire
to lend the dish a little more colour.
And the pig only kill this same morning!

They say you must eat the coucou
for the sake of the sauce

but the pudding and souse taste real good!

And of course you got plenty rum to drink with it too.
White rum and coloured rum.
Snaps.
Minis.
Half-pints.
Flasks.
Pint-an'-a-half bottles.

With ice and water.
Or without.

With a sweet drink or a beer to chase it.
Or without.
Cause this is where the rum come from

and the sweet smell of sugar settles over the land during
Crop.

Steak-fish
hot-pepper seasoned
sizzles over wood fires in Baxter's Road

and the shrill tin flute
and the beating of the drum
the beating of the drum
bass drum
snare drum
and the clatter of the steel
are the engine of the Landship
beating up the street

white uniformed members
out on manoeuvres
rolling to the rhythm

of ancestral sound

"More oil in my lamp, I pray!
Keep it burning!
Keep it burning!
Keep it burning
Till the break of day!"

The ship sails on
and the limers on the pavement
and the standers in the doorways
get back
to talking their talk.

Over in the corner the next body
telling anybody who listening
who it was they did see
in the churchyard
and who they was with
and just what they was doing

under the
frangipani trees shedding their blossoms
white
pink
blood-red.
Duppy-flowers.

And this body talking
'bout how he going to see the Minister:
"Man, I is a voter!
I is people too!
An' when I got somet'ing to tell he,
He does got to listen!"

And that body talking
'bout the cricket match they did watching
out 'pon the pasture
And how they still playing
till the light beginning to fail
and the home team win by bare six kiss-me-arse runs.

Out the back
in Debra's yard
city-bred banana trees
dapple palings with their shadows

palings shining silver
in the moonbeams
shimmering
to the nearby all-encircling sea.

–John Gilmore

To experience Barbados is to confirm all the romantic notions of "islandness" we hold so dear in Europe and America — constant sunshine, tropical beauty, and a pleasant sea-psyche that disdains petulance and shrugs off the little annoyances of life. And yet that same experience also contradicts our other island stereotypes — that island dominions are unsophisticated; that island people are passive; that island commerce is restricted to tourism. Barbados is so different from these Caribbean cliches as to be shocking. This nation's devotion to culture and education puts the rest of the world to shame; its people are among the most industrious and ambitious in North America; and its economy resonates with vitality from international trade, tourism and a rekindled spirit of of entrepreneurship.

It is a country of contrasts: sleek and modern in many ways, yet clearly still attached to the customs, traditions and religion of England; accommodating to the pace and energy of a commercial life, yet choosing a rhythm through it that feels slower and less aggressive; fearful of God in the Anglican tradition, yet without its oppressiveness.

In short, Barbados is a country as complex and diverse as any you will find anywhere. But in the attempt to know it and understand it, the newcomer to Barbados has an ally: its size. It measures only 21 miles from top to bottom, only 14 miles wide. Given time, a map and a vehicle, Barbados can be explored and revealed in hundreds of fascinating ways, even to the most languid tourist. In Barbados, life is not hidden. It is a tropical isle, after all, with an openness born of the physical reality of heat and sunshine. Its activities, interests and moods are all on the surface, outside, which makes it such a joy to be a traveller or a photographer, here in the jewel of the Caribbean Sea.

THE ISLAND

Cove Bay

St. Lucy coastline

Animal Flower Cave

Harrison's Cave

Over the waste of waters! to the isles
Where, with unfading beauty, Summer smiles;
Where, mid the splendours of the glowing west,
The happy, fables say, enjoy their rest,—
With Saturn's train, through vocal gardens rove,
Or, loitering, linger in the bowers of love;
Or, welcomed by the daughters of the deep,
In coral palaces are sung to sleep;

From *Barbadoes* by M.J. Chapman, 1833

Near Bathsheba

Near Speightstown

Bathsheba

Long Bay

East Coast

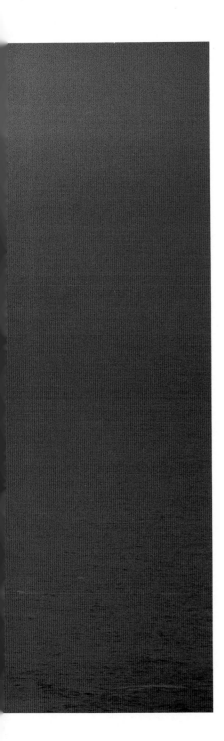

*For to confesse truly, all the Ilands that I have passed
by and seen unto this day, not any pleaseth me soe well.*

Sir Henry Colt, 1631

Crane Beach

BEACHED

The sea that contains our dark history steadily turns
its gilded pages. A man's foot stamps each fresh pain
of meaning into the burning scroll of sand.
Soon, as the tide rises, each syntax
will be blotted from memory's chapter and
this searching man must begin again.
One vowel of sunlight shoots and burns
over the gorgonic reefs. His soul heaves and grips the descending light.

Darkness too soon devours this space,
chasing him inland to the sighing chattel. The harsh fact
of an unfinished poem tightens like rope in his chest. He must rise and pace.

The child is eager to rush from the womb. The child will fight
to clutch a new pain.
Tomorrow, he will be on this beach again.

— *Anthony Kellman*

Brighton Beach

Bridgetown

Independence Arch

Trafalgar Square

Trafalgar Square

Chattel houses

How different today's Barbados is from the uninhabited island the English came upon in 1625. Having arrived first near Holetown, the English sailors, led by Captain John Powell, landed and claimed the island for King James I. Two years later, an English settling party of 90 came ashore at Holetown, and, as simply as that, the link to England was forged and the prevailing culture of the island was set for all time. As word leaked back to England of this beautiful place, Barbados became known as the New Frontier, and to its promising shores came disinherited sons of the English gentry, political refugees, adventurers, laborers, ruffians, rogues, kidnappers fleeing from the law and a sturdy group of farmers eager to start anew.

By the 1640's sugar cane had been brought to the island, and had turned a struggling agricultural economy from rags to riches. The Dutch provided the fuel for this remarkable turnaround. It was they who underwrote the making of sugar, who brought African slaves to the white planters and who paid handsomely for the sweet cane and its juice. Profits to plantation owners from these Dutch traders were huge, and the Barbadian plantation system, with its reliance on slave labour, became entrenched.

By 1675, the brutal nature of the slave economy sparked the first of many inevitable, and unsuccessful, slave revolts, the most famous of which was Bussa's Rebellion in 1816. Although put down by militia, Bussa's Rebellion can be viewed as a watershed event, for it was in the aftermath of the violence that Parliament allowed Barbados to determine its own policy of slave registration and treatment. While slavery continued long after this date, historians will agree that the cultural disposition to emancipation of the slaves was established in those years, and perhaps the momentum leading to total independence from England was irretrievably set in motion.

Of course, the long journey to independence from those early days was not a foregone conclusion. Barbados' political history has been marked by mass migrations, riots, factionalism, political infighting, worker's rights battles, strikes, wars — in short, the kinds of territorial, social and economic conflicts that typify all cultures in their movement toward maturity.

Barbados' new life began in November, 1966 when its sovereign status became official. Since that time, Barbadians have grown stronger and deeper in their independence. We see now, in these nearly 25 years of autonomy, an emerging will, and a celebration of the Bajan heritage that assures self-understanding and a sense of unity and national purpose.

THE HERITAGE

Garrison Savannah

Morgan Lewis Mill

Landship at St. James Parish Church

St. Mary's Church

St. James Parish Church

My own dear island! fairest, brightest gem
In that sea-crowning, graceful diadem,
Which royally the old Atlantic wears,
And wore in secret for a thousand years,
Till the bold Spaniard found his own bright world,
And over unknown realms his flag unfurled.
How dear to me that pearl-drop of the west!
'Twas there I hung upon my mother's breast;
'Twas there sun, moon, and stars first shone for me,
The daedal earth, and ocean's majesty;
'Twas there, from Nature's book — sea, earth and sky,
I early learned the heart's morality;

From *Barbadoes* by M.J. Chapman, 1833

St. Nicholas Abbey

St. Nicholas Abbey

Gun Hill

The Lion at Gun Hill

For as we passed along near the shore, the Plantations appeared to us one above another like several stories in stately buildings, which afforded us a large proportion of delight.

Ligon, *The True History of Barbados*, 1647

Sunbury Plantation House

Villa Nova

Villa Nova

Codrington Theological College

Sam Lord's Castle

Farley Hill

St. John's Church graveyard

Speightstown

St. Thomas Church

The English landing parties of 1625 and 1627 disembarked on a Barbados that was totally uninhabited. Upon claiming the island and discovering no signs of life, they must have felt themselves to be the island's first inhabitants. But in fact two previous cultures had survived for centuries on the island — the Arawak indians, and their probable conquerors, the Carib indians. The English settlement survived, though, where their predecessors did not, and, unlike many other Caribbean nations, only one flag, England's, has ever flown over the island. Today on this tiny gem of an island live a quarter of a million people, the majority of whom are descendants of the African slaves brought to the island to work the plantations. The rest are mostly the mixed-blood progeny of the original white English and European planters. (These whites were also in large measure responsible for populating parts of America, having migrated to settlements in North and South Carolina in the early 1700's to establish, in many cases, the slave-based agriculture of the ante-bellum South.)

Some 350 years after settlement, the Barbadian melting pot has made all of them — black, fair-skinnned and white Bajans — proud citizens of the country. As a group, no matter their ancestry, Barbadians will exhibit cultural mannerisms distinctive in the Americas: a respect for law; a love of knowledge; a quickness to wit and laughter; a resistance to anger; a reluctance to change, a preference for order and a personal warmth to match the sunny climate.

THE PEOPLE

Bathsheba

Itt is the beautyfulls't spott of ground I ever saw.

Governor James Kendall, 1690

SNAPPER

The Lane snapper roves the reef
In slow careful circles.
All those deceptive tides bring
is their illusion of filling!
Pray, child!

As he ventures out hoping for traces
of food, a bigger presence stirs.
Snapper jerks back, paces.
Rest, child!

Froth showers from underneath the *Anna Lee*
rippling the sea that glares on the reef,
tugging illusion in his deep desperate kingdom.

The animal's roots go down deep,
an anchor stayed forever.
My Love, the coral is your feeder,
the warmth of this reef, your mother.

Here, you dance, pant, moan, weep, sing.
Beyond the dipping finishing line
is death pain and parting.
There, the barracuda is waiting.
There, the shark is waiting.
Stay, child!

— Anthony Kellman

Cheapside Market

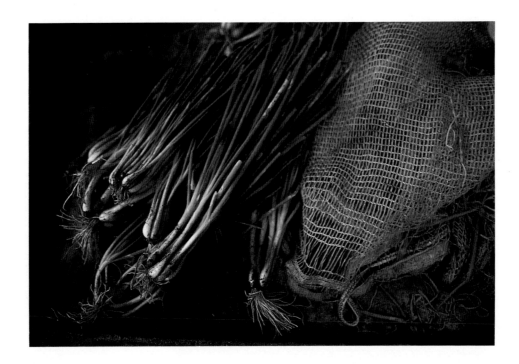

Baxter's Road

The Crane Beach Hotel

Discovery Bay Hotel

The Land lyeth high, much resembling England, more healthful than any of her Neighbors, and better agreeing with the temper of the English Nation.

From Harlow's *A Briefe Discription of the Iland of Barbados*

Colony Club Hotel

Steel band at the Casuarina Club

Ocean View Hotel

Cobblers Cove Hotel

Rockley Beach

113

Horse Racing at Garrison Savannah

Pure Sugar

Cane fields

Mount Gay Rum Refinery

ROUTE MAP

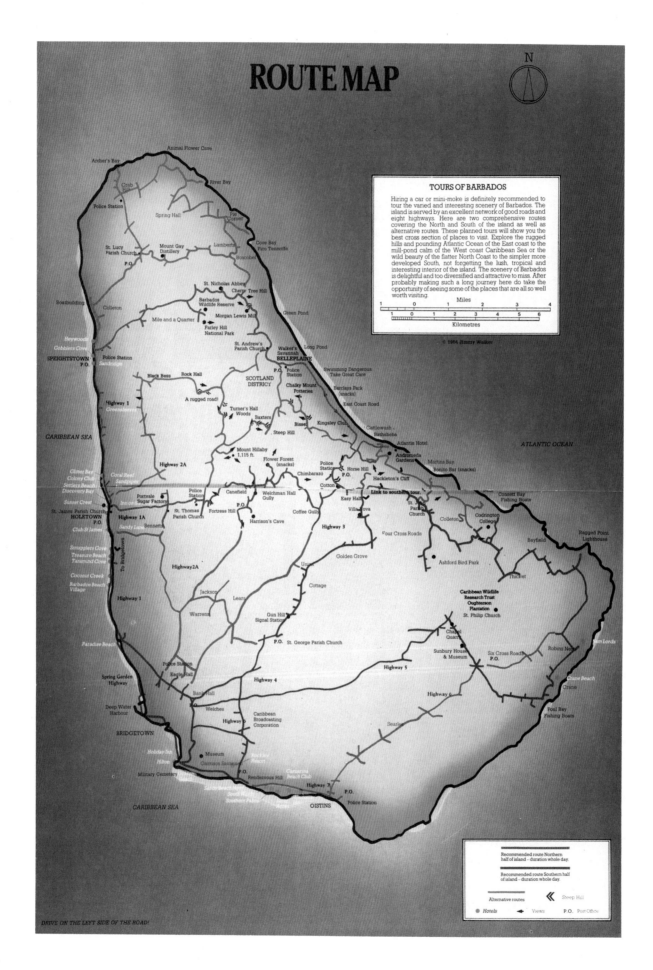

N

TOURS OF BARBADOS

Hiring a car or mini-moke is definitely recommended to tour the varied and interesting scenery of Barbados. The island is served by an excellent network of good roads and eight highways. Here are two comprehensive routes covering the North and South of the island as well as alternative routes. These planned tours will show you the best cross section of places to visit. Explore the rugged hills and pounding Atlantic Ocean of the East coast to the mill-pond calm of the West coast Caribbean Sea or the wild beauty of the flatter North Coast to the simpler more developed South, not forgetting the lush, tropical and interesting interior of the island. The scenery of Barbados is delightful and too diversified and attractive to miss. After probably making such a long journey here do take the opportunity of seeing some of the places that are all so well worth visiting.

Miles

Kilometres

© 1984 Jimmy Walker

DRIVE ON THE LEFT SIDE OF THE ROAD!

SOME FACTS ABOUT BARBADOS

Barbados is the easternmost of all the Caribbean Islands, at 13.4 degrees North and 69.37 degrees West. It lies 300 miles off the coast of Venezuela in the area of the Caribbean known as the Windward Islands.

Barbados' highest point is 1100 feet above sea level, a relatively low profile that may have prevented Spanish and Portuguese explorers from spotting it on their journeys eastward in the late 16th century.

The island measures 21 miles long and 14 miles wide, with a population of 260,000.

Its location near the equator brings sunrises around 5:30 a.m. and sunsets around 6:00 p.m. all year round.

Barbados' year-round average temperature is 80 (27c), with about 3,000 hours of sunshine. Rainfall average is about 60 inches per year, usually in sporadic showers in the "rainy" season of September, October and November. Relative humidity ranges between 60 and 70 percent. Nights are cool and pleasant on the island, with ocean breezes prevailing on the east (Atlantic) coast.

Sugar cane has been the chief agricultural crop of Barbados for over 300 years, and most of the island's tillable land is still devoted to it. Food crops make up about 12 percent of the agricultural yield, however, to help minimize food imports.

The annual summer Crop Over Festival, which begins in July, and the carnival-like Kadooment Day parade on the first Monday in August are considered Barbados' most festive occasions. Other national holidays include New Years Day (Jan. 1), Good Friday, Easter Monday and Whit Monday, May Day (May 1st), United Nations Day (first Monday in October), Independence Day (November 30), Christmas (Dec. 25), and Boxing Day (Dec. 26).

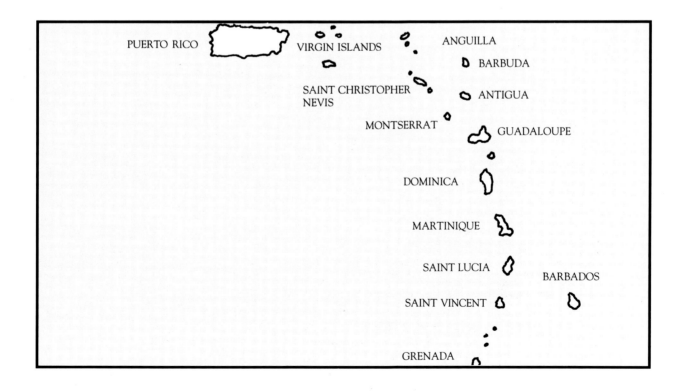

PLACES OF INTEREST

The National Stadium. Opened by H.R.H. Prince Charles in 1970, it was designed as a multi-purpose facility and can seat 5,000, with standing room for 1,000.

Sam Lord's Castle. Located in St. Philip, this beautiful mansion is the legacy of the notorious Sam Lord. A Barbadian planter, Samuel Hall Lord built the mansion in 1820. The Castle features priceless antique furnishings and paintings, mahogany columns in the living room, splendid plaster ceilings and has been wonderfully preserved. Sam Lord's Castle is now part of a luxury resort owned by Marriott's.

The Barbados Museum. A former British Military Prison, it presently houses extensive collections of Barbadian flora and fauna, Barbadian craftsmanship, porcelain and silverware, toys, dolls and games from the Victorian era, antique maps, historic portraits and landscapes, unique West Indian prints, artifacts from the period of slavery, and sugar and Amerindian artifacts from Barbados and neighboring islands.

University of the West Indies. Located on the crest of Cave Hill, this modern campus overlooks the city and Port of Bridge-town and was opened in 1963. The Cave Hill campus makes up part of the University which also has campuses in Jamaica, Trinidad and Tobago. Faculties include Law, Social Sciences, Education, Natural Sciences, Arts and General Studies. Part of the Medical Faculty is located at the Queen Elizabeth Hospital in Bridgetown.

Gun Hill Signal Station, St. George. This former British military installation has been restored by the Barbados National Trust and is a popular site for visitors.

Codrington College, St. John. Originally the home of Christopher Codrington, a Barbadian planter who at the age of 30 became Captain General and Governor of the Leeward Island. The oldest Seminary established in the Western Hemisphere, the college was founded under his will dated 1702 and opened in 1745 as a Theological College.

Villa Nova, St. John. An excellent place to capture the opulent lifestyle of 17th and 18th century Barbados. The beautifully preserved "Great House" was built in 1834 by Edmund Haynes, a successful sugar baron. Set in picturesque tropical gardens, the mansion's ownership through the years includes Sir Anthony Eden, a former British Prime Minister. Queen Elizabeth II and Prince Phillip visited Villa Nova in 1966 and planted two portlandias, renowned for their fragrant blooms.

St. James Parish Church, St. James. Near the site of the island's first settlement and among the four oldest surviving churches in Barbados, local legend claims that St. James' first ten or twelve feet from the foundations up are part of the original stone church. In fact, both the font and south entrance are over 300 years old and the church bell was cast in 1669, predating the famous Liberty Bell by 54 years. In 1982, Ronald Reagan and his wife Nancy worshipped here while on vacation, which made him the first United States President to visit Barbados.

Morgan Lewis Mill, St. Andrew. This is the only windmill remaining with its wheel house and sails in perfect working order. Dutch Jews who settled here from Brazil and pioneered both the cultivation and manufacture of cane sugar gave the windmill its strong Dutch resemblance.

St. Nicholas Abbey, St. Peter. Built around 1650, this house's curved gables are said to be of the Jacobean style. It is said to be one of only three such Plantation Great Houses of that period still standing in the Western Hemisphere. Like Villa Nova, the house is furnished with fine Barbadian and English antiques and also boasts an 1810 Coalport Dinner Service, a collection of early Wedgwood Portrait Medallions and even a black and white home movie film shot in 1935 depicting island scenes and the sugar manufacturing processes of the day. Probably built by Colonel Benjamin Beringer, ownership passed on to Sir John Yeamans who, in 1663, set out from Speightstown to colonize Carolina. Yeamans went on to become the third Governor of South Carolina.

Mount Gay Distillery, St. Lucy. The distillery has been making rum since the 1800's and produces 500,000 gallons annually. The product is shipped to Bridgetown, where it is blended, bottled and sold.

Andromeda Gardens, St. Joseph. Internationally renowned, this beautiful garden has an astonishing variety of plants from all over the tropical world and a bubbling stream meandering through, forming pools and waterfalls.

Animal Flower Cave, St. Lucy. Although the sea anemones which gave the cave its name are now few in number, the cave remains an interesting natural phenomenon on this rugged island tip.

Farley Hill National Park, St. Peter. The Park boasts a magnificent view of the East Coast and the ruins of a sugar planter's mansion. This is the place for those who prefer an idyllic stroll in shady, green gardens surrounded by brilliant blooms with now and again a glimpse of a monkey or two. The house and park grounds were filmed for the movie, "Island in the Sun."

Garrison Savannah. Formerly used as a parade ground by the British Regiment stationed there in colonial times, the Garrison is the home of thoroughbred horse racing in Barbados and hosts competitors from Trinidad, Martinique and Guadeloupe on keenly contested race days.